This book is dedicated to
Zech and Angie - chosen blessings - and their amazing families.

DEDICATED

EXTRAORDINARY

FAMILY

GIFT

G

H

HAPPY

INCLUDED

JOY

KINDNESS

Lots & Lots of Love

OUTSTANDING

PROTECTED

Understanding

Victorious

Discussion:

1. Don't wait to talk about the adoption. The longer you wait the harder it will be.

2. Discuss events surrounding the adoption. Just as kids love to hear about events surrounding their birth, adopted children want to hear about events surrounding their adoption.

3. Discuss the process in a kid-friendly, age-appropriate way.

4. Develop vocabulary pertaining to adoption: Use adopted. Many use birth mother, biological mom, etc. Educate child on what a mother is, i.e., a mother is one who not only gives birth but also is someone who loves and nurtures and cares for her child. Many things make a mother.

5. Use discussion questions such as What does adopted mean? What does it mean to belong in a family? What does respect mean to you? How can we show respect to one another? What are some reasons kids are adopted?

6. Be honest and open. Give your child permission to talk to you about the adoption at any time. Don't make your child feel bad for asking questions because of your trepidation or worries.

7. Keep a scrapbook.

8. If your child is older, she/he may need to grieve. This does not mean your child doesn't love you!

9. Seek professional help when needed. Everyone has life events and different reasons during which we could use a helping hand.

10. Play with your child; have fun together!

Made in the USA
Monee, IL
14 July 2021